MW01173982

IS YOUR DREAM REALLY WORTH IT?

Discover Your Passion, Purpose, and Plan

TONY SHAVERS III

TABLE OF CONTENTS

Dedication

THIS BOOK IS DEDICATED TO my mother, Nakia Linzie-Shavers, and my brothers, Tory and Terrell Shavers. I hope to serve as an inspiration for anything you decide to accomplish in life. Hold fast to your visions until they become a reality.

Foreword
by Tom Pinnock

TONY SHAVERS III DARES TO dream big, and as you can see, he even has the courage to write a book about it. Indeed, his wisdom and inspirational words on the following pages will go a long way in helping you realize the amazing power that resides within all of us… the power of our dreams. And yes, Tony is a dreamer, and to be honest, that's one of the things that I love the most about him.

The truth is we need more dreamers in the world like Tony. People who are willing to get out of their comfort zone, dream big, love much, and make a positive difference in the world. Throughout the following pages you will find step by step plans that will not only help you identify your dreams, but they will also show you how to put those dreams to work so that your glorious visions can become a reality.

This is a workbook, too. Tony has gone to the trouble of giving you writing assignments that will force you to look within yourself so that you can discover the true and meaningful desires of your heart. I strongly encourage you to take the time to do these assignments because it's critical that you truly understand your purpose and desires, and that you write them down. That way you can clearly see them, and that is a sure-fire way to motivate you to take action.

Years ago, I dared to dream of a new home for my wife and three young children. The little house that we lived in at the time was backed up to a swamp full of snakes and alligators. My wife, Karen, gave me a picture of a house that she dreamed of, and I placed it on my bathroom mirror. Next to it I wrote the number five. I knew that if I'd simply talk to five people a day about my business, that one day I'd have a proper home for my family. I rolled up my sleeves, went to work, and in less than two years we had a beautiful new house.

One of the many things that I like about this book is that Tony shares a number of inspirational stories about other people who dared to dream and get out of their comfort zones. I also enjoyed the many quotes from famous people, and how they used dreams combined with action to do great things. The fact is that by reading about other successful people and how they achieved their goals helps us to achieve ours.

I've always said that when it comes to dreams aim for the stars. If you do that, you'll clear the tree tops and be on your way. Tony

Shavers III has done just that with this book, and he is on his way to the stars and beyond.

Follow your passion, be prepared to

work hard and sacrifice, and above all, don't

let anyone limit your dreams."

—*Donovan Bailey*

Introduction

I WANT YOU TO TAKE five deep breaths. I'm serious, there's a method to this madness. Really allow yourself to connect to the depths of your soul. Inhale...Exhale! Inhale...Exhale! Inhale...Exhale! Inhale...Exhale! Inhale...Exhale!

Okay, did you feel some weight lifted off your shoulders? This breathing technique is important to release any built-up tension our bodies naturally fall into. By taking long, deep breaths you prime your entire body to relax. This is only the beginning. In order to determine if our dreams are really worth it, we have to be honest with ourselves.

My journey to write this book started February 22, 2017, at 2:22 A.M. While there isn't a significant importance to this time, it was quite amazing to see how creative my mind really operates.

The title of this book was actually inspired by a movie entitled Zootopia. There's a scene in the movie in which the main character expresses her interest in wanting to be the first bunny cop in town. After exclaiming her vision to her parents, they reply with, "Do you know why your mom and I are so happy? It's because we settled for life." The main character then goes on to explain that her quest to pursue her dreams is so important, and she won't stop at anything until it's achieved.

In that moment, it became clear to me that this predicament is something most people encounter. Do we pursue our dreams, or settle for what's comfortable? I posed the title of this book as a question for self-reflective purposes. While I do want to fight on your behalf for your dreams, ultimately the decision is up to you. I can't tell you if you dream is really worth it, but rather I can set the stage for what's possible and provide tips to build a strong foundation and use my personal experiences to serve as inspiration.

This book isn't for someone who reads self-help books in an endless loop, trying to find easy answers. It's for those who are finally ready to take the leap and get started. They're sick of waiting around for something to change. But they need help taking the first step, which is always the hardest. This is where my book comes in.

I'm not going to preamble, go off on tangents, or beat a message to a pulp. I'm going to offer sound bites, compelling personal stories, and exercises that easily convert to action. This is the uniqueness of my book.

Is Your Dream Really Worth It? Is for every single person who has ever wanted to live the lifestyle THEY desire.

INTRODUCTION

Is Your Dream Really Worth It? Is for the single parent who had to put their dreams aside for their children.

Is Your Dream Really Worth It? Is for the young professional working in the corporate world, but still has personal goals and is trying to find a way to do both.

Is Your Dream Really Worth It? Is for the senior citizen who has given many years to the workforce, only to retire and regret not taking more chances to pursue their passions.

Is Your Dream Really Worth It? IS FOR YOU! Your dreams are important. It's not a matter of IF your dreams can become a reality, it's just a matter of WHEN, and this book is going to help you get there.

Many of us aren't living out our designed purpose. A large majority of us have taken jobs for the paycheck, or are coasting along, hoping to win the lottery. Is our purpose really only to get by?

"What do you want to be when you grow up?" Do you remember this question? Perhaps your family member, friend, or teacher asked you this at a young age. Your answer was far-fetched, and your mind was limitless. In that moment, anything and everything was truly possible. You were innocent and carefree. The harsh opinions of others weren't allowed into your dream world. But somewhere down the road, something happened that steered us away from our dream world, and we became conditioned to believe happiness resides elsewhere.

We went on to follow a roadmap that was given to us by someone else – going to school, getting a high paying job, and retiring at 65. That spark we felt early on slowly died. Only in our later years were we puzzled by the lack of fulfillment we were promised. What was the point of it all?

Fulfillment comes in following your dreams, those things that make you excited to get out of bed in the morning. Fulfillment happens on the journey of discovering and pursuing your purpose, the one thing you can do better than anyone else in this world.

My wish for you is that you allow yourself to be vulnerable in this process. Take the things you learn and apply the ones that resonated most. My goal in creating this book was that you would be able to pick it up multiple times throughout the year and reflect on where you started as compared to where you ended up.

How many years will it take before you give yourself permission to work on your dreams?

Chapter 1

Destined 4 Greatness

TODAY, I AM AN AMAZON best-selling author, Top Ten Finalist for best self-help book from the Author Academy Awards, entrepreneur, self-publishing coach, fundraiser, and philanthropist.

While all these things sound amazing, and they are, my journey here had its ups and downs, just like everyone else. Let me just start off by saying I'm no one special. I just have a large vision for my life, and I choose not to let other people's opinions hinder my future.

I always knew I had a gift that was placed in me by God and ministered to my spirit by my mother. Since the fourth grade, I fell in love with words and the way in which imagery could touch us deep down in our souls. I knew that if I focused on my gift and constantly allowed myself the space to grow, I would accomplish phenomenal things.

But, my journey didn't start with this book or my titles. It started the moment I was born, and I think it's safe to say my story could be described as a miracle.

I was born 1 pound, 5 ounces at Alta Bates Hospital in Berkeley, CA on November 5, 1992. I was considered one of the *"miracle premature babies."* During the time of my birth, doctors told my mother I wouldn't make it through the night, and if I did, there would be complications growing up. Talk about giving up hope before solutions were even considered!

To some degree, I could understand why they felt that way. It was rare for someone born as early as I was – and weighing the same as four sticks of butter – to live, let alone thrive like any normal kid. Even though I survived this unbelievable beginning, I started encountering challenges as I grew up, but they weren't the challenges the doctors predicted. I went through a period of low self-esteem due to bullying on school campuses, along with struggling to find the inner peace to accept a non-existent relationship with my dad and the road of battling his incarceration.

Through all of this, my saving grace was poetry. It allowed me to channel all of my hurt and frustration into art. I'm reminded today that every single experience I've had has led to this moment.

I've always known I'm destined for greatness, and getting others to believe it wasn't an easy task. I've told people my dreams of becoming a millionaire so that I can give to nonprofit organizations. Some laughed and said it would never happen, while others encouraged me to always look ahead.

I know what I want for my life, and I will literally move heaven and hell to get there. My passion and purpose are to be of service to others. A lot of people describe me as passionate, and I'm not only passionate about meeting new people and learning from them, but also the work I do.

As a growing young man, I was taught to follow the traditional route of going to school, getting a high-paying job, and working in the corporate world. While I succeeded in the corporate world, I knew my other goals were just as important. The challenge was finding balance between the two. Even though I was working my nine to five job, I still had hours after work that were being wasted.

I thought to myself, "What else could I be doing with my time?" and immediately joined different community organizations to build my network. If you can get up every morning and go to work for someone else and can't devote the same amount of time to your dreams, then you don't believe in yourself enough.

I believe in myself so much that I inked my body with tattoos that read:

IS YOUR DREAM REALLY WORTH IT?

Destined 4 Greatness

Born from Words

Survived 11/05/1992

BE *Wise, Grateful, Humble, Patient, Positive, Involved, Prayerful*

These tattoos symbolize the foundation of my life. What's the foundation of yours?

You have to know, and this is super important, that every move you make aids in creating opportunities for your future self. I had a vision for my life at a young age, and still do now, and I know that even small beginnings blossom. It reminds me of one of my favorite scriptures, Zechariah 4:10: "*Do not despise the small beginnings, for the Lord rejoices to see the work begin.*"

Continue on your life's quest! Your dreams will manifest when they're meant to. Keep pushing and striving to be the best version of yourself.

The only limitations are the ones you choose to believe.

Chapter 2

Get Out of Your Comfort Zone

"Move out of your comfort zone. You can only grow if you

are willing to feel awkward and uncomfortable when you

try something new"

—*Brian Tracy*

IF I WERE TO ASK you, **"Are you living your purpose?"** would you be able to confidently answer "Yes!"?

It's easy to allow complacency to rob you of your joy. You stay in the same job, hang around the same group of folks, eat the same food, listen to the same music, and your life becomes a constant replay of the same story.

Deep down, you hunger for more, but because you don't want to step off the edge into a place of uncertainty and discomfort, you keep your feet firmly planted on the ground. Perhaps you have family members or friends who tell you, "Don't take that job." "You can't succeed in that business." "Don't take risks."

What if you could see your life five years from now, and because of the risks you took, you were provided with opportunities you couldn't fathom? **If you stay where you are, is it going to help you become the person you want to be?**

This is where we get honest with ourselves. Nothing's going to change unless we first step outside our comfort zones and ask if this is really where we want to be, and who we want to be. The first step is always the hardest, but once you take it, there's no going back.

Everyone has a purpose, even if they don't see it right now. Everyone has a dream – something they want to be working towards, or something they want to put into the world. Take a look at where you are today. It took a leap of faith to get this far, didn't it? To become even greater is going to require the same amount of awkwardness and discomfort. In order to change, you're going to have to step outside your comfort zone. If you don't, you'll fall into old habits and patterns because you're scared. It's okay to be scared, but the world (and your soul) needs you to take action anyway.

GET OUT OF YOUR COMFORT ZONE

I can't tell you what you're capable of. I can only paint the vision of what's possible. In order to create your legacy, we're going to start by looking at the stories we tell ourselves. Once we identify why we've been holding ourselves back from our dreams, we'll be able to start moving forward towards greater fulfillment, greater purpose, and greater joy.

Take some time to answer the questions below.

Question 1: What's holding me back from my dreams?

_____

_____

_____

_____

Question 2: Why am I fearful of pursuing my dreams?

_____

_____

_____

Question 3: What could be the benefit of pursuing my dreams?

_____

_____

_____

_____

_____

_____

Question 4: If my life depended on me achieving my goals, what would I do differently?

_____

_____

_____

_____

_____

Chapter 3

Three Fundamental Steps

YOU MAY BE ASKING YOURSELF, "How do I determine the steps I should take to go after my dreams? How do I find the motivation? What things can I do to help me get started?"

The answers to these questions will be unique to you and your situation. However, there are some things you can do to support your journey.

When building anything new, it's crucial to have a strong foundation. In my own journey, I've identified three important practices to keep me grounded, stay resilient, and above all, to keep me moving forward.

Here are the three fundamental practices for supporting your dreams. Make sure to complete the exercises at the end of each section to help the lessons really sink in.

1. CREATE YOUR GRATITUDE LIST

"Develop an attitude of gratitude, and give thanks for everything that happens to you, knowing that every step forward is a step towards achieving something bigger and better than your current situation."

—Brian Tracy

IN ORDER TO BUILD YOUR dreams, you need to be grateful for what you already have. This is a foundational step to turn your dreams into reality.

It's one thing to just be grateful for something, but when you have a reason behind your gratitude, it puts it into a deeper perspective. Jack Canfield has a powerful quote about forming your why. "What is the why behind everything you do? When we know this in life or design it, it's very empowering and the path is clear." Make sure to include WHY this aspect of your life made it on your gratitude list.

What Are You Grateful For? To give you an example, I've included my list:

1. I am GRATEFUL for my family, because they've been instrumental in providing feedback on my journey of going after my dreams.
2. I am GRATEFUL for my college education, as it has opened doors for me I didn't think were possible.
3. I am GRATEFUL for sunshine, because it allows me to delve deeper into my creative writing side.
4. I am GRATEFUL for my mentors, who have helped shape me into the person I am today.
5. I am GRATEFUL for poetry, because it grants me the freedom to let me mind create worlds of possibilities, and it inspires me to continue my journey of fueling my passion.

Now, it's your turn! Take five minutes to create your gratitude list. As the days go by, your list will grow, mirroring growth within yourself. Add to this list daily and repeat your gratitude list to yourself every day.

CREATING YOUR GRATITUDE LIST

1.
2.
3.
4.
5.
6.
7.
8.
9.
10.
11.
12.
13.
14.
15.

2. STOP UNDERESTIMATING YOURSELF

"Don't underestimate the power of your vision

to change the world. Whether that world is your office,

your community, an industry or a global movement,

you need to have a core belief that what you contribute

can fundamentally change the paradigm or way

of thinking about problems."

—Leroy Hood

DON'T UNDERESTIMATE THE POWER OF *your* vision to change the world. It took me about two hours to find the perfect quote to adequately explain this message. In order to accomplish your dreams, you need to stop undervaluing yourself.

IS YOUR DREAM REALLY WORTH IT?

Your mind is a powerful instrument and knowing how to control it takes a considerable amount of time and patience. The moment you tell yourself you CAN'T do something your mind shuts down all possibilities of figuring out strategies to accomplish your goals.

You have the innate ability to pursue the lifestyle you want. You just need someone or something to help you unlock the potential within.

Take a moment right now to reflect on all the ways in which someone's infinite potential touches your life every single day. Think about your computer, iPad, and cell phone. Behind those tools was a person who had a vision they wanted to turn into a reality. Imagine if that individual's self-doubt got in the way, and they chose to believe all the reasons why they couldn't accomplish something. We wouldn't have smartphones and tablets as we do today.

If you continue to doubt the greatness inside of you, the passion to fulfill your designed purpose will remain stagnant. Because you're stepping outside your comfort zone, your mind will be frightened. It will probably ask you things like:

What if no one will like it?
What if I don't succeed?
What if it takes me 10 years?

THREE FUNDAMENTAL STEPS

What if people don't invest in my talents?
What if I don't finish?

Does this sound familiar? So much of the world we live in revolves around this FEAR that our dreams and goals can't be reached!

Whether we have a solution to bring to the market or want to pursue our talents and share them with the world, our minds react by telling us it's IMPOSSIBLE.

Why? Well, it's simple... it's easier to think of reasons why our dreams can't be reached instead of the reasons why they can. I want you to think about a project or an idea you have and ask yourself why you haven't completed it. I can already tell – your mind is moving at lightning speed with answers you habitually tell yourself. Go ahead and write those answers down under the *Reasons Why You Can't* section of this chart:

IS YOUR DREAM REALLY WORTH IT?

_____ *(Write Your Project)*

Reasons Why You Can't	Reasons Why You Can

Now, next to each of the *Reasons Why You Can't*, I want you to write what the outcome would have been if you'd stuck to the project at hand in the *Reasons Why You Can*. I suspect you are having a little bit of a hard time, am I right?

THREE FUNDAMENTAL STEPS

If your *Reasons Why You Can't* outweigh your *Reasons Why You Can*, you aren't leveraging yourself and giving yourself the permission to think differently. You must get out of your head.

Listen though, I totally understand where you are. Every activity I'm having you do, I've done myself. At times, you may lose motivation to continue on your journey to fulfilling your dreams. That's a normal part of the process, and there's a simple word for it: self-doubt!

We've all felt this demon attack us at full force, especially when we've had an undeniable vision for our lives. When under self-doubt's spell, we invent and accept reasons why we CAN'T do something. In this world of chasing our dreams, we have to build an armor around ourselves, one that protects our potential for greatness from the threats of judgement and doubt.

In a similar vein, don't allow others' doubt to influence your greatness either. Later we'll dive into the importance of choosing the right relationships, but in the meantime, know that the only person who can stop you is yourself, and no one else. When you rise above your "can't" thoughts, then and only then are you walking your path to victory.

I want you to repeat the following phrase: **I AM DESTINED FOR GREATNESS!** Did you believe yourself? If not… work on saying this every single day until you believe it. You're responsible for what becomes of your life.

3. BLOCK OUT NEGATIVE THOUGHTS

"Send out a cheerful, positive greeting, and most of the time you will get back a cheerful, positive greeting. It's also true that if you send out a negative greeting, you will, in most cases, get back a negative greeting."

—*Zig Ziglar*

IT CAN BE DAUNTING TRYING to block out negative thoughts when we're confronted by them every day. You aren't alone. It takes inner strength to stay positive. I'm not saying negative thoughts won't be present, but we need to know what to do when they arise so they don't persuade us to quit.

Have you ever practiced saying affirmations? Believe it or not, they help shift our mindset to focus on things that matter. Here are a few of my favorite daily affirmations:

IS YOUR DREAM REALLY WORTH IT?

I am the architect of my life; I build its foundation and choose its contents.
I possess the qualities needed to be extremely successful.
Creative energy surges through me and leads me to new and brilliant ideas.
My efforts are being supported by the universe;
my dreams manifest into reality before my eyes.

I've had my fair share of negative dialogue that I internalized. One that I'm still learning to deal with is that I'm a young man, and sometimes people doubt my abilities and my voice. I'm self-driven and a fast learner, and if given the chance, I can show exactly what I'm capable of. But sometimes, I allow the opinions of others to seep into my consciousness, and I wonder if I should stay silent, or shouldn't try for a position. I expressed my thoughts to my mother who gave me advice that's stayed with me ever since. She said, "Son, you are the asset... not the other way around." From that moment, I knew I had a right to make my mark in the world, no matter my age.

Most of the time, our negative thoughts come from others and their own insecurities. How many times have you been shut down by family or friends when you wanted to try something new? It hurts, right? But somewhere down the road you found the courage to take control of your life. To some degree, these comments and negative thoughts are an important part of the process in moving forward with our dreams. Once we start meeting resistance, both internally

32

and externally, we know we're headed in the right direction. We're pushing past the boundaries of what's comfortable, which is exactly the path we want to be on when challenging the norms of the world. Affirmations are a tool for helping you stay the course when those voices inside and outside your head get too loud.

Along with the first affirmation below, I want you to find four other affirmations that resonate with you, write them down, and say them aloud every day.

1. *I am the architect of my life; I build its foundation and choose its contents.*

2. ....

3. ....

4. ....

5. ....

Chapter 4

Community Voices

"The one thing that you have that nobody else

has is YOU. Your voice, your mind, your story, your

vision. So, write and draw and build and play

and dance and live as only you can."

—*Neil Gaiman*

A S I BEGAN WRITING THIS chapter, I thought to myself **what would make me want to keep reading a self-help book like this?** It then dawned on me to include stories of others who are living out their purpose. The goal behind this is to let you know there are other people in the world just like you who've taken the steps to walk in their destiny.

The stories you're going to read are from my family members and friends. Each one is unique and I think you'll find them motivating and inspiring to read.

I've included their contact information and welcome you to reach out to them if anything from their story intrigues you.

Just remember, the only thing you have is YOU, and your story can also help, inspire, and encourage others to live theirs.

Nakia Linzie-Shavers

Email: thegiftlps@gmail.com
Website: www.thegiftlps.com

Scared, confused and alone. I'd finally hit rock bottom – young, divorced, caring for three young boys – and I wasn't sure how I'd go on. How was I going to rise up from such setbacks? It wasn't until I looked into my boys' eyes that I asked the more important question: "How in the world could I not?"

It was at that moment, when everything felt like it was falling apart, that I decided to follow my dreams. There were a number of things I wanted to achieve. I knew it would be a long journey, but I believed if I attacked one milestone at a time, eventually I would see the light at the end of the tunnel.

My first goal was to go back to school, and in the fall of 2006, I enrolled in junior college. The first step was to complete my general studies to obtain my AA in sociology. I knew it wouldn't be easy. Full-time student, full-time employee, and full-time mom. For eight years, with no breaks, I maintained a full course load and a 3.0 GPA. Did I experience more setbacks? Yes. Did I want to give up? Yes. Did I feel like a failure? Yes. However, in June 2014, I received my master's degree in social work with a minor in recreation. To make the occasion even sweeter, my oldest son received his bachelor's degree in sociology at the same time.

You may ask, "How did you stay motivated to do it all?" Prayer, faith, tears, and support. I prayed many nights, asking God for my purpose, my destiny. The answer was within my heart. What were my natural talents? What did I do well with little effort? What was most comfortable for me and brought me joy and fulfillment? As long as I can remember, I've always been that friend, co-worker, or family member who provided words of encouragement and another perspective when someone was having a hard time. Becoming a social worker seemed like a natural fit, and it was something I loved doing.

I'd been in hospital administration since 2006. When I graduated, I thought I'd leave the healthcare industry and blaze a new trial towards foster care and community work. Little did I know my greatest joy would come from working with families in the hospital. I've finally found my calling and my purpose in life.

When you ask yourself if your dream is really worth it, you're going to need to hold fast to what makes your dreams yours. The bible teaches us that a *good man leaves an inheritance for his children's children.* My dream is to leave a legacy that my children and grandchildren can be proud of. Inheritance is not only monetary; it's also inclusive of your values and moral compass.

Today, I'm a medical social worker and the founder of The Gift, Life Planning Services. Every day I assist individuals and families in making life decisions and creating plans for life's events.

I have a career with purpose that is limitless.

Robin Washington

Email: fleeforwomen@gmail.com
Website: www.fleeforwomen.com

I have accomplished several milestones in my life because I made a choice to push through my fears and go against the norm. One of my greatest accomplishments was homeschooling my boys. In 1988 my husband and I felt that God had called us to take this pathway with our sons.

COMMUNITY VOICES

When we started this journey, I was scared because it wasn't the popular direction at the time. But, despite all the negativity we faced from family members and friends who said we shouldn't or couldn't do this, we forged ahead. I am grateful I chose not to listen to others and continued in my faith with God. Today, I can confidently say we've raised two very successful young men and we're very proud of them.

Another great accomplishment for me was stepping into the entrepreneurial and financial arena which I've been a part of for the last 20 years. I had no formal business or financial education at the time, but I had a passion to understand how money works and how to get money to work for me. My entrepreneurial spirit was awakened in 1996 when my husband and I stepped into the network marketing industry and were able to build a six-figure income. My fascination for the financial industry developed when I learned how to become my own banker.

Many people are concerned about the financial strength of their families, but are extremely limited in their knowledge and understanding of money. Why? Typically, we don't grow up in a household where money is discussed or go through school were money is taught. My goal is to take the financial knowledge I have gained over the years and teach people how to strengthen and improve their financial position.

IS YOUR DREAM REALLY WORTH IT?

I have a passion for the financial state of women. Statistically, women are *80 percent more likely than men to be impoverished* at age 65 and older, *while women between the ages of 75 to 79 are three times more likely than men to be living in poverty.* This is why I started an organization called **F.L.E.E for Women,** (**F**inancial **L**iteracy, **E**ducation, and **E**ntrepreneurship) which focuses on empowering women to be wealthy, healthy, and financially wise. It is time for women to change the outcome of their financial future. **F.L.E.E for Women** encourages and supports women to take control of their financial well-being, so they can live a financially stress-free life.

I have learned to be thankful for every obstacle and roadblock I've encountered along my life's journey. A valuable trait that I've discovered is not to run away from my fears but forge ahead. I think in many ways my spiritual faith has brought me a long way. Listening to the Word of God on how one should conduct their life has been a guide for me to follow. It hasn't always been an easy walk, but I trust God. His word has laid a very firm foundation for the goals I've accomplished and the ones that are still in the works.

I now understand that one's dreams will always reside outside their comfort zone – outside of what's familiar.

COMMUNITY VOICES

Chris Washington

Email: clwashin@gmail.com

What is the definition of success?

This is a question that I have struggled with as I transitioned from being a child, under the protective wing of my parents, to being an adult fully responsible for my personal successes and failures in life. Life tries it's best to convince you that success is equated to money, power, and fame. However, when you look closer, you realize that none of these are a pre-requisite, or definitive outcome, of success.

Nine years ago, as I prepared to graduate college, I did not know exactly what my next step was going to be. Knowing that independence is very important to me, I knew I wanted to find a way to make money and be self-reliant. I looked for an opportunity to apply myself in a career that allowed me to apply my business acumen, competitiveness, and strategic thinking. After researching and speaking with multiple companies, I ended up accepting a job with Nestle USA. I have been fortunate to work my way up through the organization over the last nine years, culminating with becoming the highest ranking African American male within their sales organization. While Nestle is a great company with strong, historic brands, I now realize the thing that attracted me most to this career path was the opportunity to live and work in different parts of the country and, as I continue to progress, the world.

Over the past nine years I, along with my wonderful wife, Tannia and our dog, Domino, have had the opportunity to relocate to four different cities and visit parts of the country that we may never have gotten to experience. From the rolling fields of Kentucky to the glitz and glamour of Hollywood, what I have realized through this journey is no matter where you go, people that live there will tell you that it is the "best place to live." With each relocation, I have made it my objective to discover and experience whatever it is that makes the local people love where they live.

As I have continued to walk through this journey, I realize that I have begun to shape MY personal definition of success. I have discovered that what is most valuable to me is not material things, but experiences. The world is a big place, and my objective is to experience as much of it as I can with the people that I love and care about.

As you work to find and fulfill your purpose, I encourage you to first define what success looks like for you. It could be having kids, starting a company, writing a book, or teaching bible study at church. The most important part is do not let YOUR idea of success be defined by external factors. You determine what is important for your life, and then you determine to make it happen.

COMMUNITY VOICES

Nedra Smith

Email: nbsmith777@sbcglobal.net

Website: www.nedra.relivinglife.com

Today, I'm 73 years young. I'm grateful to have my own nutritional business that's allowing me to create a scholarship for less fortunate students to help them in their college endeavors, and allows me the time to work with children battling cancer.

My journey started in 1968 working for a telecommunications company called South Central Bell; a company in which I made history as the first African American to be hired. It was also the company that would let me go after 40 years working there, due to their relocating.

Like many people, especially in today's society, I became comfortable working for my employer. It, was honestly a wonderful company to work for. But with the snap of a finger, my entire livelihood was changed. I realized after working for so long that my dreams had always come second, and I knew that needed to change.

This is why I made the conscious decision to take ownership of my life and not put all of my faith in the corporate world.

If you would have told me that at 73 I would be an entrepreneur, there's no way I would've believed you. I know I have a desire to help people health-wise and financially, and today I can proudly say I've been able to do just that.

If I had to point back to an accomplishment I believe impacted my life, it would be being a grandmother. I find so much fulfillment being able to impact my grandchildren spiritually, and I get so excited when they come to me asking thought-provoking questions. Being able to now have the time to spend with them as they embark on these new journeys is so gratifying.

I believe the reason I value them so much is because of the relationship I had with my grandmother. She guided and taught me to always put God first in my life, and because of this, I've been blessed to be married for 53 years and have been able to get through many challenges.

You're never too old to start! I am definitely a living testimony. You just have to start, and then watch how everything else begins to fall into place. I have a whole new path for my life in my later years, and I'm just getting started.

COMMUNITY VOICES

Lenee Washington

Email: lenne.washington@gmail.com

Today I'm enrolled in the Urban Teachers graduate program at John Hopkins University while also teaching 2nd and 3rd graders math and science full-time in Washington, D.C. Even though this was a dream of mine, I found myself doubting my ability to teach and lead students to accomplish great things.

My passion for teaching was ignited and later confirmed through a variety of experiences in the education field. I realized I had a desire to teach while working with the Children's Defense Fund's Freedom Schools, a summer literacy program designed for minority youth. Later, my experiences at City Year, a non-profit organization that bridges the gap between what schools and teachers can provide and what students actually need, motivated me to pursue a career in teaching in order to transform the lives of students.

Embarking on this journey was important to me because of the values that were instilled in me as a child – gratitude, self-love, and spiritual guidance. These values remain pivotal in my life today.

As a child, I loved learning and engaging my mind. It has always been important to me to constantly seek a culture of learning. It's important to be able to change your perspective for the purpose of gaining new insights and results.

The journey I'm currently on has had its challenges. I soon realized that by not having a plan and spending too much time on activities that don't produce meaningful results, I needed to change. Today it's important for me to say NO when needed, to stick to the objectives at hand, and to only say YES to things that will excel my journey.

Now, at 24 years of age, everything I've learned throughout my journey has taught me that my heart has to be in my decisions. That's the only way to thrive and gain fulfillment.

Prof. Roderick K. Linzie, B.A., M.A., Ph.D.

Email: Roderick.linzie@strayer.edu

EDUCATION/CAREER: Hampton University, B.A. Strayer Univ., M.B.A (2019); The Univ. of Michigan, (M.A, Ph.D.); Professor Strayer Univ.; Adjunct Professor, Morehouse College; Clayton State Univ.; Lecturer; Clark Atlanta Univ.(Sociology.) Assist. Vice President, Dillard Univ.; Director of Graduate Admissions, Howard Univ.; Intake Ramp Manager, FedEx Corporation; Intake Specialist FEMA.

There are three essential components of leadership I've identified over the years. They are integrity, competence and effectiveness. I've learned about each from my dear relatives and ancestors, who greatly influenced my life with enduring cultural Christian values and immense sacrifice. I wouldn't be the person I am today without them, and I wouldn't have understood what I do now about the importance of sound leadership.

To me, integrity means saying what you are going to do, and doing what you have said. Word is our bond, and our word binds us. For example, my father was ill from a fatal blood transfusion of contaminated blood. But, before his death, my father asked me, "Roderick, my son, would you please take care of your mother for me?" Even at his death, he honored his commitment to his wife and family. I live each day with this commitment to Dad and Mom as our word and bond. Also, paying monthly bills and obligations are examples of integrity. Even though it was later in life when I purchased my first home (2013), I work to fulfill my bond and commitment to purchase my house—my castle in Atlanta, GA that I love. Strive to have integrity and try to own your home(s).

Competence is providing factual, accurate and informative knowledge and skills that change people's lives. When I was a graduate student, I led a team that created the Office of Minority Affairs at the University of Michigan. We created changes in the organizational structure of the university. I researched and proposed the idea of a Vice Provost for the Minority Affairs Office. I lobbied the administration. I worked to create the office before I graduated in 1993. The Office of Minority Affairs continues to exist in 2017 and has awarded millions in scholarship funding. The Office changed practices at the University of Michigan forever, even though I am no longer there.

And finally, effectiveness means problem-solving and conflict resolution. I observed a co-worker being harassed by her supervisor. I stood with her as she reported the case to Equal Employment Opportunity Commission Office/ Human Resources. It was a professional sacrifice, but I helped her to end the harassment and discrimination. Strive to be effective on organizational and personal levels. Strive to be the change you want to see. Give power to your voice and the voice of someone who lives on the margins.

Strive to be a leader that is effective, authentic and desired, because you can deliver results, and you'll improve the lives around you when you do!

Laura Thomas

Email: laura.thomasj@gmail.com

Website: www.laurathomas.life

It wasn't until I faced the greatest tragedy of my life that I decided time was too short to not follow my dreams.

I'd lived a comfortable life in the Midwestern suburbs, not for want, but also not driven by passion, and not particularly happy. Then, in 2011, my only brother and best friend was lost to suicide. I was devastated, anchorless, and suddenly painfully awake. Why was I going through life unhappy, repeating my "woe is me" story, my "I'll never amount to anything so I shouldn't even try" story? Losing Scott threw me into a stark new reality: life is precious, and we never know which day will be our last.

I started traveling the world. I wanted to know how other people found happiness, despite extreme circumstances and great tragedies. I began practicing meditation, getting to know my thoughts and creating a bit of space so I could choose to think differently. I studied psychology, seeking knowledge about the human mind, relationships, and how we could unlock the secrets to deeper connection and contentment.

Mostly importantly, I began telling stories. I'd been a storytelling for a decade, on stage, on film, and in the written form. I began writing my memoir, exploring how telling my story might be an avenue for helping others explore the pain in their hearts. I started performing my story on stage, hosting discussions afterwards about grief and its many forms. For most, the grief of not being the person they long to be hurts the deepest; deeper, even, than losing a loved one. There's nothing quite as painful as going through life not living your truth.

As I continue sharing my story, I also help others share theirs. Whether they're writing a book, crafting a speech, or creating a screenplay, they feel compelled to share something important, and I want to be there with them, cheering them on, supporting them, and helping hone their craft.

I believe stories are our oldest resource for changing the world. They give a voice to that which we find incomprehensible. They open the pockets in our hearts we keep so deeply locked away. Stories help us realize that, no matter what, we're never alone.

Losing Scott was the worst possible experience I could have imagined. And yet, it's the one that's taught me the most and encouraged me on my path of fulfilling my purpose. In truth, I never lost Scott. He still lives on in me, in the work I do, and in every interaction, I share. Scott is alive and well in my heart, and I seek to share my heart with as many people as I can.

Chapter 5

What Are You
Willing to Give Up?

---

*"Decide what you want. Decide what you
are willing to exchange for it, then, establish
your priorities and go to work."*

—*H.L Hunt*

WE ALL HAVE THE SAME 24 hours! If that's truly the case, why aren't more people living their purpose, or making plans to go after it?

Honestly, it comes down to one main thing: PRIORITY! If getting a task accomplished is truly made a priority, it's amazing how quickly the universe and our minds flip to make things happen.

IS YOUR DREAM REALLY WORTH IT?

Time is going to pass anyway, so why not put strategies in place to accomplish your goals? It's easy for us to say what we want, but when it comes to the action piece, it's as if we're waiting for someone or something to push us along. How many times have you told yourself you wanted to do something? Maybe it's drinking only water for the next 30 days. Maybe it's washing your dishes before bed each night. These are all small things, but if you can master them, everything going forward will fall into place.

I remember I had a goal to record my first poetry album when I was 19 years old called The Undeniable Truth. I had everything mapped out (venue, balloons, decorations, CD cover); the only thing that was missing was the POEMS! It hit me that none of these other things mattered unless the meat of the album was completed. I had to do some backtracking and take those small steps, which was to actually begin crafting the poems that would be featured on this album. Once that was completed, everything else took care of itself.

Because we have limited time, reprioritizing means you'll have to make space, and with that space comes sacrifice. What are you willing to give up?

Many of us have experienced the drain of a toxic relationship. There are some people who won't encourage you to follow your dreams, and might actually discourage you. It makes them uncomfortable. You're reaching new heights they've never accomplished, and it might be time to cut your ties, or take a step back from those relationships.

The same can be said when it comes to giving up something that's consuming your time, but not adding to your progress. I believe there are three things you're going to have to give up, to some degree, when pursuing your dreams:

1st: Nonproductive Activities

2nd: Friends/Inner Circle

3rd: Ineffective Time Management

Nonproductive Activities

I'm sure you have a Netflix account, or know someone who does. The average episode is about 22 minutes long, and the majority of us are into watching seasons. Let's say you watch three episodes a week. This equates to about 66 minutes of TV watching. Just imagine if you spent that time focusing on your dreams instead. Every little bit counts, and idle time is an overlooked resource that can either make your dreams come true, or make sure they never see the light of day.

Friends/Inner Circle

Have you ever heard the saying, "You become the average of the five people with whom you spend the most time with?" When you go after your goals, you'll have to face the fact that some of your friends won't be supportive. It's a difficult situation when it arises. In order to get to your destiny, you'll need to let people go. Maybe you'll choose to spend less time with them, or you'll separate entirely. We all endure this at some point in our lives. Know that walking this path of bettering your life will bring this moment into the light sooner rather than later.

Ineffective Time Management

I want you to pick up your cell phone and go to your calendar for this week and write down the times and dates you've blocked off for yourself. If you don't have any, then it's time to change this! Many of us have the purest intentions to want to improve, but if you don't make TIME for it, how can you expect anything to blossom? How many years have gone by since you told yourself "This is my year!"? You must take full responsibility for your calendar and utilize it to its fullest potential. I made it clear from the beginning that the tools I'm sharing are things I do in my personal life. And yes, there will be an opportunity for reflection following this chapter, because I believe this can be your year if you synchronize your calendar and your dreams.

Below are the three tenants of ineffective time management. I'm sure you can come up with more, and please allow yourself the space to do so. Time is the only resource you have that cannot be renewed. If we don't use our time effectively, nothing comes to fruition.

The three tenants of ineffective time management are:

Stagnation- A failure to develop, progress, or advance.

Procrastination- To put off intentionally the doing of something that should be done.

Immobility- The quality or condition of being immobile or irremovable.

How long have you been stagnant in pursuing your dreams? How long have you constantly pushed your dreams aside because it can wait until tomorrow, or you don't feel like it? How many times have you been stuck trying to figure out your next potential move?

The most important question is: Do you want to be in the same position next year?

IS YOUR DREAM REALLY WORTH IT?

If not, I want you to complete the activity below and make it a priority that you won't be in this same place, next year.

List three days out of the week where you can dedicate a minimum of 30 minutes to build your dreams?

1.

2.

3.

From the three days you selected above, write down the times during those days where you can block out 30 minutes and title the calendar event (Building My Dream)

1.

2.

3.

Now, based on the three days you chose and times for those days you allotted for your dreams, write what your dream is in the description section of the calendar event. Perhaps it's writing the hook for your music, researching personal trainers, outlining your book etc.

Chapter 6

The Power Of YES

"Always say 'yes' to the present moment...Surrender to what is. Say 'yes' to life- and see how life suddenly starts working for you rather than against you."

—Eckhart Tolle

HOW OFTEN WILL YOU CONTINUE to let fear hinder you from stepping into your greatness? You want a better life for yourself. You want to reach the end of each day and feel like you accomplished everything you could, giving the world a fist bump because of your contribution. So why are you still saying "no" to the things you want?

As you tiptoe to the edge of your cliff – off of which you'll jump to accomplish your dreams – your body reacts with fear. You don't know if this is the right move, or if you should turn back and listen to those who tell you to stay away from the edge and play it safe.

But what about your soul's yearning? What about the emptiness you feel working to support someone else's dream, but not your own?

Saying YES to going after your goals is extremely challenging. I've been blessed with so many unfathomable opportunities, and I know beyond a shadow of doubt that had it not been for me saying YES and learning along the way, I would not be the person I am today.

Let me share an example with you. In 2015, I made the decision to step into the network marketing profession, which has a bad reputation. I'd heard stories about this industry and all the scams people believe are associated with it, even though members of my family have not only been extremely successful in network marketing, but have also mentored and helped a number of people to do the same thing. I was at the cliff, peaking over the edge because this was something I knew I had a passion for – helping people understand the power of building an asset. I finally decided that taking the leap would be better than not trying at all, and my life hasn't been the same since.

I know that every new step in life does three things, which are the guiding principles for how I encourage you to look at new opportunities. Will it: 1) Grow my personal and professional development? 2) Build my network? 3) Allow me to learn from others?

If the answer is YES, those three things when a new opportunity comes your way, whether it's a music gig, new job, or a business opportunity, YOU TAKE IT!

Because I took the step off the edge of the cliff and entered a profession I'm proud to be a part of, I'm friends with doctors, lawyers, educators, multi-millionaires, authors, entrepreneurs, and motivational speakers, all because I chose to say one powerful word... YES! Worst case scenario, I told myself, I could always back away from an opportunity after checking it out. Best case scenario, I would grow by learning new things and building new friendships.

What will you do going forward to positively impact your life? How will you learn to believe in opportunities when they present themselves, and embrace them, even if they're a little scary? It's time we say YES to ourselves first and make our own opportunities before they arise. If I had waited for jobs to promote me, if I had waited for people to take me under their wings, if I had waited for someone to give me directions for my life, I would not be where I am today!

You have to put your life in your hands! Yes, if you want to discuss opportunities with your family, then by all means, do so, but understand one thing: YOU received the opportunity, not the other way around.

When you next find yourself standing on the cliff's edge, wondering if you should take the leap, know that the pounding in your heart is an indication that you've found something that excites you. You're alive, you're passionate, and you're one step closer to your dreams. It's YOUR life, and you get to choose what happens. Why not say YES?

Chapter 7

Write Your Vision &
Make It Clear

"You need to aim beyond what you are capable of.

You must develop a complete disregard for where

your abilities end. Try to do things that you're incapable

of… If you think you're incapable of running a company,

make that your aim… Make your vision of where you

want to be a reality. Nothing is impossible."

—Paul Arden

IT'S EASY TO *THINK* ABOUT what we want for our lives. We often say things like, "It would be nice to have that fancy car."

IS YOUR DREAM REALLY WORTH IT?

"It would be nice to take my children on a dream vacation." "It would be nice to pay off my college debt." Whatever the aspiration may be, we often keep it locked in our minds, never actually speaking it into existence, and never acting on it.

You have to speak your goals as if they've already been accomplished! Remember the affirmations exercise we did earlier? If you begin to project out into the world what you want, the universe will respond. You also have to be 100% clear in your vision. You may start off saying, "It would be nice to pay off my college debt." I'm sure it would be, but notice the feelings that transpire when you add a few more words commanding the attention of the universe: "My college loans WILL be paid off November 5, 2020."

See what happened there? There was a small jolt of inspiration, of possibility. I'm not saying that by writing out your vision things will magically fall into place. You still have to put the work behind it, but you have more drive to getting it done, because you aren't just keeping your projects in your head; you're sharing them with the universe, maybe even your community, and each is supporting you in the actualization of your dreams.

One of my bedroom walls says **TONY'S VISION.** Underneath are all the things I want for my life. Some are monetary, some physical, emotional, and so on. I'm speaking these things into existence as if they already are. In fact, one of the pictures has a stage, a book, and a crowd of individuals. Perhaps a book tour is in the works?

Your vision is YOURS! It was given to you for a reason. When you share your dreams with others, they might not understand what you're doing or why. That's okay. Let them sort out their dreams, and don't let their opinions stop you.

One of my favorite tools is a vision board. I'm sure you know what that is, so I won't go into detail. If you've never done a vision board, or you have in the past, I'd strongly encourage you to create one today! Our priorities change over time, and I'm of the opinion that you can't have too many vision boards. They track your shifting priorities and dreams, and help keep you focused.

For my first vision board, I used words from magazines. It read:

Success starts with ME.

I'm going to experience the art of expression to unforgettable moments

To find the place outside, that matches the spirit inside.
The dream landscape equal to the inner spirit.

I am going to have no responsibilities except to indulge in this
Technicolor sunset and connect the horizon.

IS YOUR DREAM REALLY WORTH IT?

Do you see how this world has so much room for everyone?
Have you ever seen any other world?

When you arrive, you'll know you've arrived.

I am Destined 4 My Best!

Creating this vision board set the foundation for the trajectory of my life and my purpose. I want that same clarity for you.

Below is your opportunity to create your VISION! Don't limit yourself… just allow yourself space to breathe and space to imagine all possibilities. Below you'll write out four goals you want to accomplish in six months, one year, and five years. Keep in mind that we think we can accomplish more in one day than we actually can, but we highly under predict what we can accomplish in a year. Don't be shy. Dream big, and use this as a template to map out your action steps.

WRITE YOUR VISION & MAKE IT CLEAR

_____'s Vision Board

My Goals

6 Months	1 Year	5 Year

Chapter 8

YOU Hold the Key to Your Future

"Most people are defined by their titles,

their cars, and their house, where they came from,

their color, their race, and their religion. And so, it's up

to you to take control of your own life and define you.

As long as you understand who you are, you will have

a solid foundation of understanding what your

talents are and what your skills are."

—*Stedman Graham*

WHEN ALL IS SAID AND done, the only person responsible for shaping your life is YOU! While it may be tempting to blame others and shift responsibility away from yourself, deep down you know beyond a shadow of a doubt who's in charge. In the end, you're the only one who hurts by neglecting responsibility.

I can't begin to tell you, the number of individuals I've met throughout my life who've yet to discover and fulfill their potential and live out their dreams.

I want to provide you with two very important things to consider as you go out and build your goals and help change the world with your talents and gifts given only unto YOU!

1st: Understand Your Value

If someone was to ask you, "What value do you have in this world?" would you be able to answer them immediately? If you don't know the value you bring, how can you honestly expect anyone to take you seriously? This is not to be cocky or sound as if you're above anyone, but you have a gift that others are waiting to hear. Find it. Define it. Understand it.

2ⁿᵈ: Network on Purpose

I cannot begin to stress how important this is. For some, this may be easier than others. A great way to network with others and meet new people is to attend Meetup groups in your area based on topics that interest you. You never know how instrumental a person can be in your life. I have an army of individuals in my network who've become dear friends and represent many walks of life. In the end, it all comes down to the relationships you cultivate. When you keep others at an arms distance, you create more harm than good, mostly for yourself. Open your heart. Invite people in.

It should scare you to get older and realize you've been playing it safe. Great rewards are saved for individuals who are willing to take chances and give life their all. In just a short period of working, I've held several positions that have helped me not only enhance my life, but also enhance the lives of others by creating meaningful connections. It's not always how can someone better you, but how can you better someone else.

We all have a role in society with something great to offer, something the world desperately needs. When we truly accept it, we're unstoppable. The key to your future, starts with you walking in your destiny!

YOUR FUTURE QUESTIONNAIRE

Question 1: How much time outside your day job do you work on building your dreams?

_____

_____

Question 2: How can you simplify your life and focus on things that will truly make you happy?

_____

_____

_____

_____

_____

_____

Question 3: What do you owe yourself?

_____

_____

_____

_____

_____

Question 4: In one word, what's standing between you and your biggest goal?

_____

Question 5 Where are you wasting time and energy?

_____

_____

_____

_____

_____

Chapter 9

It Won't Be Easy,
But It Will Be Worth It!

"Believe me, my journey has not been a simple journey of progress. There have been many ups and downs, and it is the choices that I made at each of those times that have helped shape what I have achieved."

—Satya Nadella

IMAGINE IF YOU HAD EVERYTHING you ever wished, dreamed, and hoped for, given to you the moment you asked. You may feel a little excited in the moment, but when reality hits, your appreciation won't linger because you didn't put in "sweat equity."

IS YOUR DREAM REALLY WORTH IT?

When you can say that due to your hard work and dedication, you were able to accomplish another task on your bucket list, you're fueled to go out and do more.

It's just like walking the stage at your high school or college graduation. For four years you went through a treacherous journey of ups and downs, trying to stay the course because you had an end goal is sight; one you couldn't really see when you first got to high school or college. You just knew what the end goal was.

You have to adopt the same drive when it comes to your dreams and aspirations. The success stories you hear are born because someone chose to stick to the everyday grind, no matter how hard the road got. When the gloomy days come, perseverance pushed them to the finish line.

Following this page is an opportunity to reflect on the times when your journey isn't easy. It might not be the most comfortable thing, facing these questions, but I want you to answer them honestly. Only when we know what caused us to stumble can we prepare for the inevitable lows, and not allow ourselves to be thrown off course.

SELF- REFLECTION

Question 1: How do you need to change to accomplish your goals?

_____

_____

_____

_____

_____

Question 2: What motivates you in your lowest moments?

_____

_____

_____

_____

IS YOUR DREAM REALLY WORTH IT?

Question 3: What bad habits do you want to cut?

_____

_____

_____

_____

_____

_____

_____

Chapter 10

Take Action Today

"I've learned that our fear limits us and our vision.

It serves as blinders to what may be just a few steps down

the road for us. The journey is valuable, but believe in your

talents, your abilities, and your self-worth can empower

you to walk down an even brighter path."

—*Soledad O' Brien*

CONGRATULATIONS! YOU'VE MADE IT TO the end. You're destined for greatness, and you owe it to yourself to stop playing small. The world needs people who fearlessly fight for their dreams.

IS YOUR DREAM REALLY WORTH IT?

We're all born with a gift. Every day requires a new commitment to starting, and once you find your gift, it's time to take that first step. Believe in yourself and your dreams. I think your dreams are worth it. Do you? Ultimately, only you can answer that question.

Many of us have a desire to build our dreams, but we lack direction. Writing this book allowed me to also work on myself and my goals. I'm not perfect, and I don't have the world figured out. However, I believe in myself and that I can accomplish whatever I set my mind to.

Most of us tend to equate success with money, but it's so much more than that. Success is the IMPACT you make, either for yourself, your family, or your community. Who have you inspired, and how have you made a difference in their lives? Sometimes it's through monetary means that we make those impacts, and other times it's being a helping hand or a shoulder to cry on.

Following this page, I would like you to write a letter to your future self, ONE YEAR from now. Don't hold back! Allow yourself the time and energy to create your lifestyle. You've done the first part by reading this book, but in order to truly discover your PASSION, PURPOSE, and PLAN, you have to apply the principles you've picked up along the way.

YOU HOLD THE KEY TO YOUR FUTURE

To connect with me online and share testimonials about how this book has blessed your life, please connect with me at:

Instagram: tonyshavers_3

Facebook: Tony Shavers III Consulting

Tiktok: tonyshavers_3

Email: info@tshavers.com

Website: www.tshavers.com

Letter to Yourself

___/___/___

Dear _____,

Made in the USA
Columbia, SC
23 April 2023

15548407R00050